D0914959

LMH Official Dictionary of

JAMAICAN
WORDS &
PROVERBS

Compiled by
L. Mike Henry / K. Sean Harris

© 2002 LMH Publishing Limited
First Edition
10 9 8 7 6 5 4 3 2 1
2003 Revised
10 9 8 7 6 5 4 3 2
2006 Revised
10 9 8 7 6 5 4

All rights reserved. No part of this book may be reproduced, stored in a retrieval system, or transmitted, in any form or by any means, electronic, mechanical, photocopying, recording, or otherwise, without the prior written permission of the publishers or author.

The publishers have made every effort to trace the copyright holders but if they have inadvertently overlooked any, they will be pleased to make the necessary arrangements at the first opportunity.

If you have bought this book without a cover you should be aware that it is "stolen" property. The publishers and author have not received any payment for the "stripped" book, if it is printed without their authorization.

All LMH titles, imprints and distributed lines are available at special quantity discounts for bulk purchases for sales promotions, premiums, fund-raising, educational or institutional use.

Compiled by: L. Mike Henry / K. Sean Harris
Cover Design: Susan Lee-Quee
Illustrator: Clovis Brown
Design & Typesetting: Michelle M. Mitchell

Published by: LMH Publishing Limited
7 Norman Road,
Sagicor Industrial Complex
Building 10
Kingston C.S.O., Jamaica
Tel: 876-938-0005; 938-0712
Fax: 876-759-8752
Email: lmhbookpublishing@cwjamaica.com

Printed in China

ISBN: 978-976-8184-30-◼

Publisher's Notes

LMH Publishing is pleased to produce the first eleven books in a series of titles which will treat the Jamaican culture in a serious yet entertaining format.

The first eleven titles in this series are:

- LMH Official Dictionary of Jamaican Words & Proverbs
- LMH Official Dictionary of Popular Jamaican Phrases
- LMH Official Dictionary of Jamaican History
- LMH Official Dictionary of Jamaican Herbs & Medicinal Plants and their uses.
- LMH Official Dictionary of Caribbean Herbs & Medicinal Plants and their uses.
- LMH Official Dictionary of Sex Island Style
- LMH Official Dictionary of Sex Island Style Vol. 2
- LMH Official Dictionary of Caribbean Exotic Fruits
- LMH Official Dictionary of Jamaican Religious Practices & Revival Cults
- LMH Official Dictionary of Bahamian Words and Proverbs
- LMH Official Dictionary of Popular Bahamian Phrases

As this series cannot be complete without the response of our readers (as no other publisher has yet attempted to record our culture) we implore you, our readers, to voice your opinions, comments and observations which we will take into consideration when publishing new editions.

I hope you enjoy our witty and innovative series. See you next time.

Mike Henry
Publisher

ABBREVIATIONS USED IN THE TEXT

adj.	adjective
adv.	adverb
conj.	conjunction
interj.	interjection
n.	noun
v.	verb
phr.	phrase
prep.	preposition
pron.	pronoun
illus.	illustrations

A

This letter often times replaces the "h" in Jamaican talk. For instance, "De wuk 'ard yuh see!" The work is very hard.

Acktapuss, *n.* Octopus.

Actoba, *n.* October.

Ahoa, *adv.* Used to emphasize. "Mi nah go wid yuh, ahoa!" I am definitely not going with you. *(illus.)*

Aise, *n.* Ears. "Mi aise nuh big." I don't have big ears.

Aldoah, *conj.* Although.

Annadah, *adj.* Another. "Sell mi annadah slice a cheese." Sell me another slice of cheese.

A nuh nutten, *n. phr.* It's no big deal. Unimportant.

Appie, *adj.* Happy. "'Ow come yuh so appie?" Why are you so happy?

Areddi, *adv.* Already. "She gawn areddi." She is already gone.

Arinj, *n*. Orange. Citrus fruit. "Mi a go pick cupple arinj." I am going to pick a couple of oranges.

'At, *v*. Refers to both hot or hat. "It really 'at tidday!" It's really hot today.

'Ave, *v*. Have. "Mi 'ave money." I have money.

Awrite, *adj*. Okay. "Yuh awrite?" Are you okay?

Ax, *v*. Ask. "Nuh ax mi nutten." Don't ask me anything.

Bawn, *v.* Born. "She neva bawn inna hospital." She
was not born in a hospital.

Badda, *v.* Bother. "Don't badda fi go." Don't bother
to go.

Bade, *v.* To have a bath.

Baddie, *n.* Body.

Bad wud, *n. phr.* Expletive; Curse word.

Baggie, *n.* Panties. *(illus.)*

Bandulu, *v.* Swindle.

Baps, *adj.* Used to show suddenness. "Mi a walk
good den next t'ing mi jus' baps an' fall dung!"
I was walking okay then I suddenly fell down.

Bangarang, *n.* A loud noise or commotion.

Bashy, *adj.* Fabulous; Nice. "Dah dress deh bashy."
That's a nice dress.

Batty, *n.* Bum, ass or backside. In Jamaica, to be
told that you have a big "batty" is a
compliment. (Females of course)

Batty man, *n. phr*. A homosexual.

Baybie, *n*. Baby.

Baybie madda, *n. phr*. The mother of one's baby. "Mi baybie madda nuh stop ax fi money." My baby's mother is always asking me for money.

Bawl, *v*. Cry; Holler.

Beenie, *adj*. Tiny; Small.

Ben dung, *v*. Bend down. "Ben dung low." Bend down low.

Benchas, *n*. A reserve player for a team; usually a soccer player.

Behine, *n*. Behind; Rump. Also used in annoyance. "Yuh behine man!"

Begga, *n*. Beggar.

Betta, *adj*. Better. "Dis yah much betta." This is much better.

Big up, *v. phr*. "Big up yuh chess mi fren'!" A phrase used in greeting someone in a respectful yet informal way.

Billias, *adj*. Full of gas (bodily).

Bisnis, *n*. Business.

Blacka, *n*. Nickname given to a guy of very dark complexion. Usually sticks for life.

Blabba mout, *n*. Person who talks too much.

Bless, *n. adj.* A form of salutation used by many young Jamaicans, particularly those of the Rastafarian faith. Also used to indicate that all is well. "Everyt'ing bless man!" Everything is fine.

Blood claat, *conj*. Expletive used to exclaim about something.

Blouse an' skirt, *n. phr*. An exclamation; usually used when excited about something.

Boasy, *adj*. Flamboyant. "'Im boasy eeh." He's very flashy.

Bokkle, *n*. Bottle.

Boots, *n*. Condom; Rubber.

Bootie, *n*. High top shoes.

Brawta, *n*. Extra; Bonus.

Bredda, *n*. Brother; Friend. "Yes mi bredda!" This greeting could either refer to one's biological brother or just a friend.

Brownin', *n*. A light coloured girl. Usually has no shortage of admirers.

Bruk out, *n. phr*. To become loose or unruly. "Eva since de gal madda dead she jus bruk out." Ever since her mother died, she has become very loose.

Bud, *n*. Bird. "Look pon dah bud deh." Look at that bird. Also if you're told that you have "bud leg", that means that you have skinny legs.

Buddy, *n*. Penis. Generally used by teenagers.

Bumbo claat, *n. phr.* A curse word that is usually used in anger but is sometimes used when one is surprised or startled.

Bumpa, *n.* Bumper; Female butt. "Mi bumpa 'ave a dent", as in vehicle or, "De gal bumpa big nuh raas!", as in a woman's buttocks.

Butta, *n.* Butter. "Put mo butta pon mi bread." Put more butter on my bread.

Buttafly, *n.* Sexy Jamaican dance. Be warned, one may get aroused watching the local girls doing this move.

Butu, *n.* A stupid person, especially from a rural area. City folk are disdainful of stupid country folk.

Buzz mi, *v. phr.* Call me.

Bwile, *v.* To boil. "Bwile some wata." Boil some water. Also "She mek mi blood bwile!" She made me furious.

Bwoy, *n.* Boy. Can be used to greet a friend of any age, but to address a stranger like this, will most likely get you a hard punch to the face or worse.

Caa, *v.* Can't. "Mi caa go." I can't go.

Caal, *v.* Call.

Cabin stabbin', *v. phr.* To have sex. A local hit song made the phrase popular.

Cerfitikate, *n.* Certificate. "Mi caa fine mi birt' cerfitikate." I cannot find my birth certificate.

Cha cha bwoy, *n. phr.* Well dressed man.

Chaklit, *n.* Chocolate. "Chaklit" tea is very popular with rural folks.

Chaka chaka, *adj. phr.* Extremely untidy. "'Ow yuh 'ouse so chaka chaka?" Expressing disgust at someone's untidiness.

Chat, *n.* Talk.

Check, *v.* To go see somebody. "'Im a go check yuh later." He's going to visit you later.

Chi chi man, *n. phr.* A homosexual.

Challis, *n*. Apparatus used to smoke marijuana. Generally used by most Rastafarians, who smoke marijuana religiously. A little reminder to our visitors, marijuana is illegal.

Chiney brush, *n*. Liquid which is brushed onto the penis to increase staying power. For those with erectile dysfunction.

Chiney shop, *n*. Shop owned by someone of Chinese ancestry.

Choosday, *n*. Tuesday.

Chups, *v*. Kiss.

Chuck, *n*. or *v*. Truck; Also to shove "Mi chuck de bwoy inna 'im face." I shoved the boy in his face. Locals take this very seriously, "chuck" someone, you better be ready for a fight.

Claat, *n*. Cloth; Also used as a curse word. *See "blood claat".*

Clappas, *n*. Fire crackers. Mostly heard during Christmas and New Year's Eve celebrations.

Cocky, *n*. Penis. *See "buddy".*

Coolie, *n*. An East Indian. Reputed to have "white liva." Meaning they are sexually insatiable.

Coodeh, *v*. Look at that.

Cotch, *v.* To support; To stay. On a bus if someone begs you a "cotch" he wants to share your seat. If you are home and someone begs you a "cotch", that is of a more serious nature as they asking you to put them up. (usually indefinitely)

Cova, *v.* or *n.* Cover. "Cova yuh mout'" Cover your mouth. Also "Weh di pat cova deh?" Where is the cover for the pot?

Craven, *adj.* Greedy. *See "gravalishus".*

Cris, *adj.* Pretty; Fine; Okay. "Dah 'ouse deh cris" That's a pretty house.

Curry, *n.* A spicy seasoning used to flavour chicken and mutton. Curry goat is a delicious and popular Jamaican dish.

Curry favour, *v. phr.* To be biased towards someone, for example: a mother treating one of her children better than she treats the rest.

Cut eye, *v. phr.* To look maliciously at someone. To "cut eye" at someone could get you into an argument.

Cutliss, *n.* Machete. If you make someone angry and they say that they're going to get "dem cutliss" you better haul ass. *(illus.)*

Cya, *v.* Carry.

Cyar, *n.* Car.

D

Dat, *pron.* That. "Jus' look at dat." Just look at that.

Daise, *n.* Days.

Dem, *pron.* Them. "Mi nuh chat to dem!" I don't talk to them.

De, definite article. The. "Yuh si de dawg?" Have you seen the dog?

Depon, *v. phr.* Plans. "Weh yuh depon tomorrow?" What are you doing tomorrow?

Dese, *pron.* These. "Mi waan dese." I want these.

Deyah, *adv.* Here. "Mi deyah." I am here.

Did, *v.* Jamaicans use the word did to show past tense. "Mi did go laas night." I went last night.

Dideh, *adv.* There. "It dideh man." It's there.

Dinna, *n.* Dinner. In Jamaica, Sunday "dinna" is usually the best for the week. A lot of preparation goes into it.

Dis, *pron.* or *n.* This; Also disrespect. "Dis yah a fi mi book." This book is mine. Also "De bwoy dis mi star!" The boy disrespected me.

Do, *v.* Asking for a favour; Please. "Do, mi a beg yuh fi a dolla?"

Doah, *adv.* Don't. "Doah play wid mi." Don't play with me.

Docta, *n.* Doctor.

Dose, *pron.* Those; Also to sleep briefly.

Draw Crowd, *n. phr.* When an event attracts a lot of spectators, it "draw crowd", meaning many people attended.

Dread, *n.* A Rastafarian.

Dressa, *n.* Dresser.

Drop pan, *n.* A local gambling game.

Dun, *v.* Done; Finished. "Mi dun read de book." I've finished reading the book.

Dun grow, *adj. phr.* Term used to describe midgets, dwarfs or any really short person.

Dung, *v.* or *n.* Down. "Mi a go dung deh." I am going down there.

Duppy, *n.* Ghost; Apparition. "Mi si wah duppy yessiday." I saw a ghost yesterday. Telling "duppy stories" is a popular pastime of elderly rural folk.

Dutchie, *n.* Pot used for cooking.

Dutty, *adj.* Dirty; Filthy. "De 'ouse dutty eeh?" The house is very dirty.

Dutty wine, *n*. The latest dance craze out of Jamaica. It involves moving the waist in sexually suggestive manner while simultaneously moving the head in a wild circular fashion. For women only. No man should be caught dead doing the "dutty wine".

Ê

Eeeh? *adv.* A response like yeah or huh? *(illus.)*

Eeena, *adj*. Inside. "She neva come eeena de cyar." She never came inside the car.

Ef, *conj*. If "Ef yuh dweet, mi a go pay yuh." If you do it, I'll pay you.

'Ello, *interj*. Hello.

Faas, *adj*. Fast; Inquisitive. "Mine yuh bisnis, yuh too faas!" Mind your business, you are too nosy.

Face bwoy, *n*. A handsome fellow.

Facety, *adj*. Rude or disrespectful. "De likkle bwoy facety yuh si!" The little boy is so rude!

Fah, *prep*. For. "A weh she want mi fah?" What does she want me for?

Fallah, *v*. Follow. "Fallah mi up de road." Follow me up the street.

Fallah fashin, *adj. phr*. This phrase is used to describe people who love to emulate or try to do things exactly like somebody else. "Yuh too fallah fashin!" You like to follow too much.

Fambly, *n*. Family. "Mi fambly a go pon wah trip." My family is going on a trip.

Fambly ram, *n. phr*. A male who commits incest. Such persons, when exposed, are usually exiled from their communities, especially in the rural areas.

Fassy 'ole, *n. phr*. Someone who acts unreasonably or unfairly. You hear someone yell, "Ah wah fassy 'ole dat eenuh!" somebody has wronged him.

Fatta, *n.* Nickname given to a fat or obese male. If one remains heavy, this name will most likely stick for life.

Fava, *n.* Favor; Resemble. "'Im fava 'im daddy eeh?" He resembles his father. Also use to curse "Yuh face fava!" You are ugly!

Finga, *n.* Finger. "She cut 'im finga!" She cut his finger.

Fix, *v.* Other than the traditional meanings, to "fix" someone is to put a curse on them. This practice is called "obeah".

Flowas, *n.* Flowers. "Mi a go buy flowas fi de living room." I'm going to buy flowers for the living room.

Fren, *n.* Friend. "A mi big fren dat!" That's my very good friend.

Fresh, *adj.* This has several meanings. "De likkle bwoy fresh yuh see!" The little boy acts too grown-up or rude. "Mi a sell fresh fish" means that the fish is literally fresh. "De food too fresh" means that it needs more salt.

Fyah, *n.* Fire.

Fyah bun! *v. phr.* To emphatically denounce someone or something. "Fya bun fi higher prices!" Denouncing a hike in prices.

Full 'undred, *n. phr.* High praises; The whole information. "Gi mi de full 'undred bout wah 'appen." Tell me everything that happened.

G

Gallang, *v.* Go on. "Gallang a yuh yaad!" Go to your yard.

Gallis, *n.* Male with many girlfriends; Promiscuous. Local hit song popularized the word.

Ganja, *n.* Marijuana; Pot; Weed. Revered and smoked religiously by Rastafarians. Still illegal in Jamaica.

Gangalee, *n.* Don; Gangster.

Ganzy, *n.* A casual shirt. Usually knitted, perfect for the heat.

Gimme, *v.* Give me. "Gimme t'ree slices." Give me three slices.

Ginga, *n.* Ginger. "Ginga" tea is a good remedy for bellyache.

Ginnal, *n.* Con-man; Trickster.

Glamity, *adj.* Vagina that is considered good. "She 'ave de glamity!" Sex is good with her.

Glaas, *n.* Glass. "Mi a go bruk up de glaas!" I'm going to break the glass.

Glaas bokkle, *n. phr.* Refers to any bottle made of glass.

Go weh, *v. phr.* Go away. Usually used in anger. "Bwoy go weh fram yah so!" Boy, go away from here! *(illus.)*

Go deh, *v. phr.* Go there. "Mi a go deh Sunday." I'm going there on Sunday.

Gravalishus, *adj.* Gluttonous; Greedy. See "craven".

Gree, *v.* Agree. "Mi an' 'im neva 'gree 'bout nutten." He and I has never agreed about anything.

Grine, *v.* Grind. Traditional meanings aside, telling a female that you would like to "grine" her, means that you would like to have sex with her.

Guzum, *n.* A spell; Magic.

Gwaan, *v.* Go on. "Yuh gwaan, mi soon come." You go on, I'll soon come. Can also be used as encouragement. "Gwaan my bwoy!" Spurring someone on.

Gwine, *v.* Going to do something. "Mi gwine heet now." I'm going to eat now.

Haffi, *v.* Have to. "Yuh haffi go tidday." You have to go today.

Hail, *v.* Simply means to greet someone. "Hail up yuh madda fi mi." Tell your mother hi for me.

Halla, *v.* Holler. "Weh yuh a halla out mi name fah?" Why are you hollering out my name?

Hangle, *n.* or *v.* Handle. "De door hangle bruk." The door handle is broken. "Hangle yuh bisness." Handle your business.

Hask, *v.* Ask. *See "ax".*

Haas tonic, *n.* Horse tonic. A drink that is believed to increase virility in men. *(illus.)*

Hat, *adj.* Hat; Also hot. "Tidday hat sah!" Today is very hot. *See "at".*

Heet, *v.* To eat. "Heet all a yuh dinna!" Eat all your dinner. *See "nyam".*

24

Hegg, *n.* Egg.

Heng, *v.* Hang. "'Im sentance fi heng." He was sentenced to hang.

Higgla, *n.* Street vendor. Seen all over the island peddling various wares.

Hile, *n.* Oil. Also if someone says that his "hile a ride 'im" that means he hasn't had sex in a long time.

Hype, *v, adj.* Used to describe anyone or anything that is exciting. "Di movie did hype!" The movie was exciting.

Idiat, *n*. Idiot.

Idrin, *n*. Friend. "A mi idrin dat." That is my friend. *See "fren".*

Igle, *adj*. Idle. "Dah bwoy deh igle yuh see!" That boy is so idle. Generally refers to guys who just hang out and don't work or go to school.

Im, *pron*. Him. "Doah go wid 'im!" Do not go with him.

Inna, *prep*. In; Into. "She live inna big 'ouse now." She lives in a big house now.

Infahmah, *n*. Informer; Snitch. Ever heard the term "snitches get stitches?" Well that is apt here, nobody likes a snitch.

Instead ah, *adv. phr*. "Instead ah mi go tomorrow, mi a go tidday." Rather than or instead of going tomorrow, I'll go today.

Irie, *adj*. Cool, Okay; Nice. "Yuh irie?" Are you okay?

J

Jah, *n.* God. Term usually used by Rastafarians. It's typical to hear them shout "Yes Jah!"

Jeezam, *n.* An expression used to convey surprise and amazement.

Jizzle, *n.* Drizzle; Light rain.

Jan cro', *n.* John Crow, which is the name of the local buzzard. Also used to describe people for whom you have the utmost contempt.

Jook, *v.* To stick. "De pin jook mi." I got stuck by the pin.

Junju, *n.* Fungus. Also if someone says you have "junju mout'", you have a nasty mouth.

Kawn, *n*. Corn. "Mi a go buy some kawn." I'm going to buy some corn. Boiled corn eaten with butter is very delicious.

Kawz, *n*. or *v*. Cause. "A kawz a yuh mek it 'appen." It's your fault why it happened.

Ketch, *v*. Catch. "Mek we go ketch some fish." Let's catch some fish.

Kibba, *v*. Shut. "Kibba yuh mout'." Shut your mouth. It would be the smart move to heed this warning.

Kine, *adj*. Kind. "'Im kine yuh see!" He is so kind.

Kip, *v*. Keep. "Kip yuh money kawz mi nuh waan none." Keep your money cause I don't want any.

Kotch, *v*. To lean against. *See "cotch"*.

Kriss, *adj* Nice; Pretty. "What a kriss cyar!" What a pretty car.

Laas, *v.* Lost. "De pickney laas 'im suda." The child lost his pacifier.

Labba labba, *adj. phr.* Talkative. "She too labba labba!" She talks too much.

Lan', *n.* Land. "Mi a save fi buy lan' so mi can mek mi 'ouse." I am saving to buy land so that I can build my house.

Lang, *adj.* Long. "'Im gone lang time." He has been gone for a long time.

Lang mout', *adj. phr.* If you have a "lang mout'," you are pouting or you envy other people.

Lawd, *n.* Lord. "Lawd mi caa tek it nuh mo" is a popular expression. Lord I can't it anymore. Also "lawd 'ave mercy."

Lef, *n.* Leave. "Mi say fi lef mi alone!" I said to leave me alone. Could also mean left, the opposite of right.

Leggo, *v.* Let go. "Leggo mi han'!" Let go of my
hand.

Lickie lickie, *adj. phr.* Greedy. "Yuh too lickie
lickie!" You are too greedy!
See "gravalishus". (illus.)

Lickle, *adj.* Little; Small.

Linga, *v.* Linger.
"Doah linga inna de doorway."
Don't linger in the doorway.

33

Macca tree, *n*. A prickly plant.

Madda, *n*. Mother. "Tidday a maddas day!" Today is mother's day.

Maggle, *n*. Model; To show off. "Mi pickney waan fi maggle when she get olda." My child wants to model when she gets older.

Mampi, *n*. An extremely fat woman. Be careful, she will take offense to this less than flattering name.

Mannish, *adj*. To behave like a man. Usually said to a young boy acting grown.

Marina, *n*. Tank top; Under shirt.

Mash up, *v. phr*. To break or destroy something; Also refers to someone who used to be affluent and is now destitute.

Mawga, *n*. Meagre; Skinny. "She mawga sah!" She is so skinny. Women don't appreciate this term, they would rather be referred to as slim and trim.

Mawnin', *n.* Morning. "A mawnin' arredi?" Is it morning already? Also as a greeting, "Mawnin' sah," good morning sir.

Mek, *v.* Make. "She a go mek it tidday." She is going to make it today.

Mesh, *n.* or *v.* Just right; Compatible; A knitted shirt.

Mi, *pron.* Mine. "A fi mi own!" It is mine.

Missa, *n.* Mister. A polite form of address for men. "'Ole on deh Missa Ken." Hold on Mr. Ken.

Mo, *adj.* More. "Mi waan mo food!" I want more food.

Mo fyah, *n. phr.* More fire. An expression of excitement. One might be at a party and hear a favourite song, and shout "mo fyah!"

Mout', *n.* Mouth. "'Im mout' big eeh man!" This could mean that you literally have a big mouth or that you talk too much.

Mumma, *n.* Mother. I wouldn't advise you to use this one though, some people don't like this term and might think you're being flippant.

Mussa, *v.* Must be. "Yuh mussa idiat!" You must be an idiot.

Naa, *adv*. No; Not. "Mi naa go." I'm not going.

Nable 'tring, *n. phr*. Navel string. When Jamaicans say their "nable 'tring" cut at a certain place, that means they love that place like home.

Natty, *n*. or *adj*. Knotted; Dreadlocks.

Nedda, *adj*. Another. "Gi mi a nedda one." Give me another one.

Neegle, *n*. Needle. "She 'ave neegle yeye pum-pum." That means she has a tight vagina. (Hence the analogy needle eye.)

Neva, *adv*. Never. "Mi neva a go back deh!" I'm never going back there.

Nex', *adj*. or *adv*. Next. If you're in line somewhere and someone yells "nex'" you better move it before you get a tongue lashing.

Nize, *n.* Noise. "Tap de nize pickney!" Stop the noise child!

Nookie, *n. phr.* Yet another word for the vagina.

Nose 'ole, *n. phr.* Those two holes above the mouth that you breathe through. Known in some places as nostrils.

Nuff Respect, *n. phr.* Utmost respect. A very popular term heard anywhere on the island.

Nuh watch nutten, *v. phr.* Don't worry about a thing. *(illus.)*

Nutten, *n.* Nothing.

Nyam, *v.* Eat. "Yuh nyam too much." You eat too much. *See "heet".*

Obeah, *n.* Black magic; To put a spell on someone. The "obeah man" is usually feared and respected in his community. After all, who wants to get hexed?

Ooman, *n.* Woman. "Mi is a big ooman!" Meaning she's grown so don't get fresh.

One, indef article. "Yuh see one red cyar drive pass?" Did you see a red car drive by?

One-one, *adv.* Separate. A popular saying is one-one cocoa full basket.

Ongle, *adj.* Only. "A ongle one lef." There is only one left.

Ooo, *pron.* Who. "A ooo tek mi book?" Who took my book?

'Ouse, *n.* House. "Dah 'ouse deh big eeh!" That's a really big house!

Outta, *adv.* Out of "Tek it outta de fridge." Take it out of the fridge.

Ova, *prep.* Over. "Gwaan ova deh." Go over there.

Pawt, *n*. Part. "Mi ongle see de laas pawt." I only saw the last part.

Paypa, *n*. Paper. "Write it pon a piece ah paypa." Write it on a piece of paper. Also refers to newspaper.

Peas head, *adj*. This is an insult, as it refers to the shape of one's head or the type of hair one has; so make sure that you only say this to someone you know and as a joke.

Peppa, *n*. Pepper. Black pepper is a popular seasoning among Jamaicans. "Mi love when de food peppa!" I love when my food has lots of pepper.

Piece, *n*. Traditional meanings aside, telling a female that you want a "piece" means that you're asking for sex. So be careful, if you don't know her she will be offended.

Pickie Pickie, *adj. phr.* Extremely selective; Choosey. "Tek weh yuh get, yuh too pickie pickie!" Take whatever you get, you're too choosey.

Pickney, *n.* A young child. "A fi yuh pickney dat?" Is that your child?

Plague, *v.* "Mi plague wid headache." I have a serious headache.

Play play, *adj.* To pretend. Little boys play "cowboys and indians" or G.I. Joe. Little girls play with their dolls and pretend to be mommy.

Poas, *v.* Mail; Post. "Mi wi poas de letta tidday." I will mail the letter today.

Pown, *n.* Pound. "Sell mi a pown ah flour." Sell me a pound of flour.

Pudung, *v.* Put down. "Pudung mi plate!" Put down my plate.

Pum-Pum, *n.* Vagina.

Punani, *n.* Another colourful term for the much loved female anatomy. (vagina)

Puppa, *n.* Father. "Mi puppa naa come back." My father is not coming back.

Quashie, *adj.* Poor; Destitute. "A ooo yah chat to 'ole quashie?" A local cutie might say this (in a derisive tone) to some poor guy whom she thinks is beneath her.

Quarrelsome, *adj.* Very disagreeable, always ready for an argument. *See "war boat".*

Quatty, *n.* Penny. The money is obselete but the term is still used, especially by elderly folk. "Not even quatty mi 'ave fi gi yuh." I don't have not even a penny to give you. *(illus.)*

43

Raatid, *n*. A slightly profane exclamation that you should only use in informal settings.

Radda, *adv*. Rather. "Mi radda dweet now." I'd rather do it now.

Ramp, *v*. Play. "Mi naa ramp wid yuh!" I'm not playing with you.

Raas, *n*. An extremely popular curse word which is used in anger as well as in jest.

Rasta, *n*. Short for Rastafarian.

Renk, *adj*. Rude; A foul smell such as that of urine. If you're told that you smell "renk", you need to immediately take a shower and change your clothes, because you are stinking!

Res', *v*. Rest. If someone says "res' de argument", that means to stop arguing.

Riva, *n*. River. If someone who lives in a rural community knows how to swim, most likely they learned to in a river.

Robut, *n.* An illegal taxi or bus. They are not licensed to operate as public transport.

Rubbas, *n.* Condoms. *See "boots". (illus.)*

Ruff, *adj.* Rough. Can also mean that something was good "De movie did ruff star!" It was a good movie.

Ruff neck, *adj. phr.* Tough guy. The type of guy you don't want to tangle with.

Riddim, *n.* Rhythm; Beat. "Dah riddim yah bashy!" This is a nice beat.

Sacks, *n*. Socks.

Satday, *n*. Saturday.

Sawlt, *n*. Bad luck. When somebody laments "mi sawlt yuh see!" They are experiencing bad luck.

Sawta, *n*. Sort of. "'Im sawta cute." He is sort of cute.

Sawf, *adj*. Soft. "De ice cream too sawf." The ice cream is too soft.

Screechie, *n*. A Jamaican dance move. You have to be very flexible to master this one.

Seh, *v*. Say. "Weh yuh a seh?" Is a form of greeting.

Seh wah, *v. phr*. Say what. To exclaim in excitement. If a DJ plays a song and the crowd goes in a frenzy, he might stop the record and shout "seh wah!"

Shawt, *adj*. Short.

Shawty, *n*. Nickname given to a short person, usually male.

Shawt-ah-patience, *adj. phr.* Such an individual is very impatient and quick to blow his top.

Shotta, *n.* A respected street person.

Shet, *v.* Shut.

Shuga, *n.* Sugar. "Shuga an' wata" is sometimes given to someone who might be feeling queasy and dizzy.

Shut, *n.* Shirt.

Si mi? *n. phr.* You understand?

Siddung, *v.* Sit down. "Siddung an' be quiet." Sit down and be quiet.

Sinting, *n.* Something.

Sista, *n.* Sister. "Mi big sista a cook dinna." My big sister is cooking dinner.

Skylark, *v.* Idle; To waste time. "Pickney tap skylark an' go read yuh book!" Child stop wasting time and go read a book!

Smaddy, *n.* Somebody. "Mi a go 'urt smaddy!" I'm going to hurt somebody.

Soun', *adj. or n.* Sound. Usually refers to the sound systems that play at local dances.

Soun' bwoy, *n*. Disc jockey. Some of them are extremely popular and their parties are always well attended.

Spliff, *n*. Marijuana rolled in paper like cigarettes.

Star, *n*. Guy; Man; Friend. "What a gwaan star." What's going on man? Also the name of a local newspaper.

Stoosh, *adj*. Prim and proper. "She gwaan too stoosh man!" She acts too prim and proper.

Stone, *n*. A hard object (resembles a small stone) which is rubbed onto the penis to increase staying power. As you can imagine, it's quite popular with most men.

Suda, *n*. Pacifier.

Sweetheart, *n*. This is the lover that you would not like your significant other to find out about.

Sweet talk, *n*. or *v*. This is when one attempts to be charming, usually when you want something. For instance a vendor might say to a young lady walking by, "Pretty girl mek mi sell yuh one dress." He calls her pretty to entice her to purchase the dress.

Tail part, *n.* When you have come to the "tail part" of something you have come to the end of it.

Tallawah, *adj.* Strong. "'Im likkle but 'im tallawah!" He is small but strong.

Tandeh, *v.* Stand there; Stay there.

Tanks, *n.* Thanks. "Yuh mus' always give t'anks." You must always give thanks.

Taylah, *n.* Tailor. Jamaican school children wear uniforms to school and during the summer, most "taylahs" do brisk business making new uniforms.

Teef, *n.* Thief. Held in contempt by almost everybody. Accusing someone of being a "teef" with no proof, could result in bodily harm.

Teet', *n.* Teeth. The expression "Mi nuh skin teet'," means that I don't play around or that I don't laugh too much.

Tek, *v.* Take. "Mi caa tek it nuh mo." I can't take it anymore.

Terteen, *n.* Thirteen.

Terty, *n.* Thirty.

T'ick, *adj.* Thick. "Yuh head too t'ick" means that you're not too smart and "De gal t'ick nuh raas" means that she is well endowed in the thighs and buttocks.

T'ink, *v.* Think. "She t'ink seh mi nuh know." She thinks that I don't know.

T'ing, *n.* Thing. Usually said with an 's' even when speaking about a single thing. "Gimme mi t'ings!" Give me my things. Could be anything or any amount.

Ting deh, *n. phr.* This term is the replacement for whatever one can't remember. Could be someone's name, for instance "Ting deh seh yuh mus caal 'im." Whats his name, says that you must call him.

Trace, *v.* To use profanity when arguing.

Trash out, *adj.* Wearing the latest styles; Well dressed. "'Im always trash out." He's always well dressed.

T'ree, *n.* Three. "Mi 'ave t'ree marbles." I have three marbles.

T'row, *v.* Throw. "T'row de ball." Throw the ball.

True-true, *adj*. Authentic. "Yuh nuh true-true yardie." You're not a real Jamaican. *(illus.)*

Tump, *n*. Thump; Punch. "'Im get tump inna 'im face." He got punched in his face.

Tun, *v*. Turn. "Tun roun' bwoy!" Turn around boy!

Tursday, *n*. Thursday.

Unda, *prep*. Under. "Look unda de bed." Look under the bed.

Unda mi nose, *n. phr*. Right before your very eyes.

'Undred, *n*. Hundred. "Gi mi 'undred dolla nuh." Give me a hundred dollars.

Unnu, *n*. All of you. "A unnu mek mi sad." All of you made me sad.

Upstairs house, *n*. A house with more than one storey. Status symbol in Jamaica.

Urrycane, *n*. Hurricane.

Usban, *n*. Husband. "Mi usban naa come." My husband is not coming.

V

Vaas, *n*. Vase.

Vagaban, *n*. Vagabond. "'Im a ole vagaban." He wanders all over the place. *(illus.)*

Vampiah, *n*. Vampire. "Mi a watch a vampiah show." I'm watching a vampire movie.

Varandah, *n*. Patio; Porch. Best place to be after dinner on a cool Sunday evening.

Vencha, *v*. Venture.

Wah, *pron*. What. "A wah?" What is it?

War boat, *n*. Person that's always looking for a fight; Quarrelsome. "Mary a ole war boat." Mary is always up for a fight.

Wash out, *v*. To be flooded out of your house; To take a laxative.

Wata, *n*. Water. Also to tell a female "Yuh waan wata har garden" means you would like to have sex with her.

Weh, *adv*. Where. "Weh yuh a go?" Where are you going?

Wensday, *n*. Wednesday.

Wid, *prep*. With. "Mi naa go wid yuh." I'm not going with you.

Wifey, *n*. Wife; Significant other. The opposite of sweetheart.

Winjie, *adj*. Tiny; Small. *See "beenie".*

Winta, *n*. Winter. "A winta time inna 'merica." It's winter time in America.

Wooda, *v.* Would have. "She wooda haffi buy it back!" She would have to buy it back.

Wud, *n.* Word.

Wuk, *v.* or *n.* Work. "'Im drap outta school an' naa wuk." He dropped out of school and he's not working.

Wus, *adj.* Worse. "De sore pon mi leg a get wus." The sore on my leg is getting worse.

Wut, *adv.* Worth. "Yuh nuh wut it." You are not worth it. *(illus.)*

Yah, *adv*. Here. "Mi a stay right yah!" I'm staying right here.

Yessiday, *n*. Yesterday.

Yeye, *n*. Eye. "Mi yeye a hat mi." My eyes are hurting me. Also when someone has "puss yeye" that means their eyes resemble that of a cat.

Yuh, *pron*. You. Used in almost every sentence regardless of subject matter.

Yush, *interj*. An informal greeting.

Zeen, *v*. Okay; That's cool. "Zeen mi idrin!" Okay my friend. *(illus.)*

Zed. Z, last letter in the alphabet.

Popular Jamaican Sayings & Proverbs

Ole fyah stick easy fi ketch.
When former lovers meet, sparks might fly.

We run t'ings, t'ings nuh run we.
Being in control.

If yuh coop did clean de cock would not stray.
If the sex was good, the man would not cheat.

Wah sweet nanny goat a go run 'im belly.
The same thing that makes you happy, can make you sad.

Yuh clean de talk an' lef de wispa.
Doing things halfway.

Fowl feed a yaad nuh 'ard fi ketch.
If the places you frequent are known, you won't be hard to find.

Tedeh fi mi, tomorrow fi yuh.
Every dog has his day.

Puss an dawg nuh 'ave de same luck.
Different strokes for different folks.

Yuh play wid puppy, puppy lick yuh face.
Play with fire, you will get burnt.

Doah heng yuh basket higha dan yuh can reach it.
Live within your means.

Si mi an' come live wid mi a two diffrant sinting.
Things are not always what it seems.

If yuh live inna glass ouse doah t'row stones.
Do to others as you would have do unto you.

When wata t'row weh it cyan pick up back.
What's done is done.

When dawg flea bite yuh, yuh haffi cratch.
Every action causes a reaction.

If vuh want good, yuh nose affi run.
To accomplish certain things, you have to sacrifice.

One one cocoa fill basket.
Slow and steady gets the job done.

If yuh caan ketch quacao, yuh ketch 'im shut.
If you can't catch someone or something, catch the next best thing.

Everyday bucket go a well, bottom boun' fi drop out.
Over use of something will destroy it.

Dutty wata can out fyah.
Everything has its usefulness.

A nuh all duppy tu'n rollin' calf.
Don't stereotype people.

Same ting weh tick sheep, tick goat.
The same thing that happened to someone, could happen to you.

Trouble nuh set like rain.
Trouble can be unpredictable.

Yuh t'ink a one day monkey waan wife.
Don't be ungrateful.

A nuh everything good fi eat, good fi talk.
Not everything one hears, should be repeated.

If fish come fram deep sea an' tell yuh say it deep, yuh caan say a lie.
Don't speak about things of which you have no knowledge.

Doah t'row weh yuh stick before yuh finish cross de wata.
Don't count your chickens before they hatch.

A nuh same day leaf drop a wata battam it rotten.
Success doesn't happen overnight.

If Jan cro waan go a lan, sea breeze blow im a likkle fasta.
Be prepared when opportunity knocks.

Dawg nuh nyam dawg.
There is honour amongst thieves.

When head pawt stunted, kibba yuh mout.
Don't pretend to be someone you're not.

Gi laff fi peas soup.
Idling while there is work to be done.

Lang pass draw seat, shawt pass draw blood.
Shortcuts are never generally safe.

Scornful dawg nyam dutty pudding.
Don't be too choosy.

Dem a carry straw.
They are having a loving affair.

Howdy panky bruck nuh square.
Its good to be polite.

Doah truble truble, till truble truble yuh.
Avoid mischief.

Every jan cro' t'ink 'im pickney white.
Parents think the best of their kids.

Cow seh bacra wuk neva done, mule say it mus dun.
One's temperament helps decide how difficult a job is.

When dawg a sleep nuh wake 'im.
Don't stir up trouble.

If yuh get ole a de blade, cayfull 'ow yuh draw eh.
Proceed cautiously in a dangerous situation.

When horse dead, cow get fat.
Regardless of the circumstance, somebody benefits.

Duppy know who fi frighten.
Bullies never pick on someone their own size.

Likkle canoe kip near shore.
It is wise to stay within safe limits.

Cock mout' kill cock.
Betray oneself with careless chatter.

Yuh caan siddung pon cow back so, an' cuss cow 'kin.
Don't take kindness for granted.

When plantain waan dead it shoot.
To show off one's self.

Jackass who gellup an kick, mus' get cucoomacca tick.
One who misbehaves, must be punished.

Rain a fall but di dutty tough.
Although outwards appearances are fine, times are hard.

When man igle 'im go a pastcha go tell cow howdy do.
The devil finds work for idle hands.

When cockroach give party, 'im nuh ask fowl.
Be careful of the company you keep.

When dawg 'ave money, 'im buy cheese.
When one has money, one can be indulgent.

Yuh ketch cow by 'im awn, but man by his wud.
Watch your words, for they might come back to haunt you.

Tail a de laas t'ing any dawg shoulda chase.
Do unto others as you would have them do unto you.

Yuh caa plant kawn an' expect peas fi grow.
You reap what you sow.

Chief inna town, ginal mus' live.
As long as there are fools there will always be unscrupulous persons to take advantage.

Boasy nuh a cock chicken.
Behaving as though the world belongs to you.

Bad luck wus dan obeah.
Misfortune is very unpleasant.

Time langa dan rope.
Time heals all wounds.

Tek milk out a cawfe.
A skillful theif.

Bruk calabash, bring new one.
If one destroys anything, one should replace it.

Blackbud lef 'im ticks fi pick, an' pick fi cow own.
Performing an act of true unselfishness.

De bline 'ave nutten but 'im tick.
Refering to one's most dependable if not sole possession.

Empty bag caan tan up.
A hungry person cannot work efficiently.

Like a jan crow inna picherie.
Making someone very uncomfortable.

When bull ole yuh tek plantin trash fi tie 'im.
More often than not humiliation comes with old age.

Quashie come a town.

Someone in a new and uncomfortable situation.

Dress to puss-foot.

Dressed in bright colours with improper fitting.

Siddung pon 'im battam.

Lazy and unproductive.

Quatty buy trouble, 'undred poun' caa pay fi it.

Big trouble sometimes arise from the simplest of circumstances.

Yuh caa get 'ouse, yuh affi tan unda cow belly fi save mawnin dew.

One should learn to make the best of any circumstance.

When bokkle hole rum, kawntick get drunk.

Bad example corrupts anyone, particularly children.

Chicken merry, hawk deh near.

Happiness in the face of unknown danger.

Dawg wid too much owna sleep widout bone.

It's not only moral to keep only one wife, it also ensures good treatment for the husband.

One day busha a busha.

King, if even for a day.

Fishaman neva seh 'im fish t'ink.
**A salesman never points out the fault of the
commodity he is handling.**

Step like puss pon 'at brick.
Walking in a haughty manner.

*Go backra cow pen fi count cow, nuh drink 'im milk; but
when yuh drink 'im milk, nuh count 'im cow.*
Attend to the work at hand.

Nuh draw mi tongue.
Don't provoke me to quarrel.

Wha drop offa head drop pon shoulder.
From every act someone derives benefit.

Slow lacka pawson a go a hell.
In a disgustingly slow manner.

Tek 'im aise mek piss-pot.
Treat someone in an in-considerate manner.

Rock stone a riva battom nuh know sun 'at.
**Those of the privileged class experience no hard
times.**

Swap black dawg fi monkey.
Get the worse of a bargain.

High seat kill Miss Thomas puss.
Beware of exalted company.

Weh de horse tie, a deh 'im nyam grass.

A man must eke out an existence wherever he finds himself.

When one door shut anneda one open.

Don't despair because the way out of a jam is closed; there is always another.

Massa awse, massa grass.

It dosen't matter what is used because all the expense is borne by one person.

Yuh mout' a fly like sick nayga batty.

You are talking far too much.

While de grass a grow, de awse a starve.

Although the future looks bright the present is none too good.

If yuh nuh mash ants yuh nuh see 'im guts.

When someone is offended he generally airs pent up grievances.

Cow seh, tan up nuh mean res'.

Because the cow is a cud-chewing animal it is working even while standing still, so never be taken in by appearances.

De higha de monkey clime de more 'im expose imself

It is wise not to be a show-off, because everyone has a skeleton in the closet.

Man 'ave raw meat, 'im look fyah.
   It is only logical for one to seek solutions to one's problems.

Count like Jew, gree like bredda.
   To be serious in business in spite of friendship.

Like when washa ooman look pon dutty clothes a Monday mawnin time.
   To look at in a disdainful manner.

When cow tail cut off God almighty brush fly.
   God takes care of us all.

What a man nuh know olda dan 'im.
   Experience teaches wisdom.

Cuss-cuss nuh bore hole inna man 'kin.
   Quarrels do no physical harm.

If yuh neva put on ledda, yuh wooden know how boots pinch.
   We all learn by bitter experience.

Pawson crissen 'im pickney fuss.
   It is human to attend to one's interest before that of any other.

Pudden caa bake widout fyah.
   You need the right tools to do a job.

De more yuh chop breadfruit, de more it spring.
   Things grow under the right conditions.

When cotton tree tumble dung, mawga dawg jump ova it.
There is a time and place for everything.

Hungry man seh cane nuh 'ave joint.
Beggars can't be choosers.

If yuh want half a bread beg smaddy buy it, but if yuh want a whole one, buy it yuhself.
If you want a thing done the way you want it, do it yourself.

Fish a deep wata nuh know 'ow fish a riva-side feel.
There is no substitute for experience.

Peppa bun 'at, but it good fi curry.
Everything has its usefulness.

Alligator lay egg, but 'im nuh fowl.
Things are not always what they seem to be.

When jan cro' fly too high, 'im fedda drop.
Don't try to be someone you're not.

'Im 'ave jan cro' stomach.
Is not easily upset.

Man appoint, God dissappint.
While making plans remember God's will.

Nuh drive fly from anneda man cow 'kin.
Never interfere with other people's business.

Wantie wantie nuh 'ave it, avie avie nuh want it.
Those in dire need are more appreciative.

Pig ax 'im mumma, 'wha mek yuh mout' so lang?' Pig mumma ansa, "yuh a grow, yuh wi learn."

    Experience teaches wisdom.

If yuh nuh go a man fyah side, yuh nuh know 'ow much fyah 'tick bwile 'im pot.

    You can only know someone's personal affairs by getting close to them.

Crab walk too much 'im lose 'im claw; 'im nuh walk 'im nuh fat.

    Damned if you do, damned if you don't.

Tricks in trade, matches box in business.

    The layman must pay dearly to get inside information on any given subject.

Bokkle widout taper belong a cockroach.

    Guard your possession lest it become common property.

God bless pichie pachie but de devil help tear all.

    It is better to wear patched garments than to be so lazy as to use pins to hold tears together.

Gi yuh basket fi carry wata.

    Set an extremely difficult and time consuming task.

Silent riva run deep.

    A quiet person should not be taken for a fool.

Kill two bud wid one stone.
Performing two errands at the same time.

Every fish inna sea a nuh shark.
Don't paint everyone with the same brush.

Chicken dinna caa mek up fi bruk hegg.
You can't turn back the hands of time.

Too much callaloo mek peppa-pot soup bitta.
Too much of a good thing can spoil everything.

Fine out weh wata walk go a punkin belly.
Set an impossible task.

Ooo laugh laas, laughs best.
Don't be angry because someone laughs at you.
Your day will come.

When cockroach give pawty, 'im nuh ask fowl.
Mind your own business.

When shillin ole, dem call 'im ten cents.
There's a time and place for everything.

When yuh low dawg fi tase fowl hegg, 'im nyam de very shell an all.
Give them an inch, they will take a mile.

When trouble tek yuh pickney shut fit yuh.
When in trouble the smallest of assisance is
appreciated.

When bull get ole yuh tek plantain bark lead him.

**When one gets old the weakest of person can lead
him.**

Beg wata nuh boil cow 'kin.

Whatever one receives is not enough.

Puss belly full him sey ratta batti stink.

**One can afford to be critical of others when all is
well with him.**

Whe nuh hair nuh deh, nuh put nuh razor deh.

Don't go looking for trouble.